صحيح البخاري ﻦ

كتاب الرقاق

THE BOOK OF
Heart Softeners

Shaykh Muhammad ibn Salih Al-Uthaymeen

Explanation of Sahih Al-Bukhari- The Book of Heart Softeners

ISBN 978-0-61570-739-6

Foreword

بسم الله الرحمن الرحيم

In the name of Allah, the Most Merciful and Most Compassionate. Praise to the One Who completed this religion and sent guidance through His Messenger *salAllahu 'alayhi wa sallam*. To begin:

Every so often our daily lives preoccupy us and turn us away from Allah's promise. When we walk out of our homes, turn on the radio, TV, or Internet, we are distracted by the evils we see and hear. As result of immorality and unashamed disobedience, our hearts grow hard and distant from Allah and His Messenger's call. We know the message of Islam is true, but we are weak due to the rigidity of our heart, spirit and mind. In times like these, we need something to penetrate that stiffness. We need a remedy to soften that hardness and the inflexibility of our choices.

Disunity and harshness afflicts this Ummah today. Consequently, many people have turned away from brotherhood, caring, and even Islam itself. Their hearts have transformed into dwellings of complete hatred for a sinner, disdain toward the weak Muslim, and jealousy of their successful brother or sister.

I have selected some ahaadeeth from the most authentic book after the Qur'aan to soften the hearts in our chests. I used Shaykh Muhammad ibn Saalih Al-'Uthaymeen's explanations for the ahaadeeth selected. The ahaadeeth selected come from a book in Imam Al-Bukhari's collection titled *Riqaq:* Heart Softeners. This chapter brings tears to one's eyes, fear to one's mind, and most importantly it diminishes the rigidity in one's heart. I ask Allah to make the translation and compilation solely for His pleasure. I pray to Allah for acceptance of this deed and His mercy in the Hereafter.

Abu Aaliyah Abdullah ibn Dwight Battle
Ramadan 18th, 1433
Doha, Qatar ©

Table of Contents

Health and Leisure

عَنِ ابْنِ عَبَّاسٍ ـ رضى الله عنهما قَالَ قَالَ النَّبِيُّ صلى الله عليه وسلم ـ
نِعْمَتَانِ مَغْبُونٌ فِيهِمَا كَثِيرٌ مِنَ النَّاسِ، الصِّحَّةُ وَالْفَرَاغُ

Ibn 'Abbaas radhi Allahu 'anhumaa narrated the Prophet salAllahu 'alayhi wa sallam said, *"There are two blessings many people lose: Health and free time."*[1]

Explanation

The chapter *Riqaq* is a collection of ahaadeeth that refine the heart. Sometimes the heart becomes hard due to disobedience and constant carelessness, and thus needs something to soften it. The scholars have called the things that soften the heart *"riqaq."*

The Prophet *salAllahu 'alayhi wa sallam* spoke the truth about two blessings many of us lose: the benefit of our health and free time.

Many days pass Man by while he has energy and good health. No doubt this is the devil's deception, but he doesn't realize it until he becomes ill. Then he says, "Why didn't I do such-and-such when I was healthy?" "How did these days pass me by?"

Then there is free time. A person works and his provisions come to him easily. He doesn't need to search for a job to support himself. After some time, he finds himself preoccupied with seeking work and other means of support. This is when he realizes he was cheated out of his free time, as he didn't accomplish anything.

For that reason, the Prophet *salAllahu 'alayhi wa sallam* said, "There are two blessings which many people lose…"

---

[1] (5933)

1

We learn that some people don't lose the advantage of free time or good health. These people are grounded and determined, fully appreciate their health and time, and are aware of these bounties. Furthermore, they understand that times passes faster than they can conceive.

How many people put off death for a long time, and then all of sudden it comes to them? How many people are careless about a blessing, and then one day it disappears?

While someone is in sound health he says, "When I'm old, I won't have the ability to work." Then suddenly he's afflicted with a chronic illness that prevents him from working.

This is the way of this life, and no one is safe from it, so one must be farsighted. This is similar to the speech of the Prophet *salAllahu 'alayhi wa sallam, "Take from your good health before your sickness and your life before your death."*

The Example of this Life in contrast to the Hereafter

اعْلَمُوا أَنَّمَا الْحَيَاةُ الدُّنْيَا لَعِبٌ وَلَهْوٌ وَزِينَةٌ وَتَفَاخُرٌ بَيْنَكُمْ وَتَكَاثُرٌ فِي الْأَمْوَالِ
وَالْأَوْلَادِ ۖ كَمَثَلِ غَيْثٍ أَعْجَبَ الْكُفَّارَ نَبَاتُهُ ثُمَّ يَهِيجُ فَتَرَاهُ مُصْفَرًّا ثُمَّ يَكُونُ حُطَامًا
وَفِي الْآخِرَةِ عَذَابٌ شَدِيدٌ وَمَغْفِرَةٌ مِنَ اللَّهِ وَرِضْوَانٌ ۚ وَمَا الْحَيَاةُ الدُّنْيَا إِلَّا مَتَاعُ
الْغُرُورِ

Know that the life of this world is only play and amusement, pomp and mutual boasting among you, and rivalry in respect of wealth and children. Its likeness is as vegetation after rain: thereof the growth is pleasing to the tiller, then it dries up and you see it turning yellow; then it becomes straw. But in the Hereafter (there is) a severe torment (for the disbelievers, evil-doers), and (there is) forgiveness from Allah and (His) Good Pleasure (for the believers, good-doers), whereas the life of this world is only a deceptive enjoyment.[2]

Explanation

Allah the Most High explains in these verses that the life of this world is play and amusement. Play for the body, amusement of the heart and outward splendor. Along with this world is the boasting of the tongue.

A man may boast and brag to another, "We have more money and children than you." Everyone says, *"I am more than you in wealth and stronger in respect of men."* (Al-Kahf: 34). These people resemble an abundant rain that amazes the tiller, and afterwards the vegetation grows, but afterward it dries up. It's been said the tillers are disbelievers because

---

[2] (Al-Hadid 20)

3

nothing amazes them from this world except this physical landscape. Additionally, it's been said that the man plowing is an ascetic.

"Afterward it dries up..." This means that his vegetation dissolves after it was growing fresh.

"... and you see it turning yellow..." it becomes yellow.

"... then it becomes straw..." It turns to straw in his hands and under his feet. This is like the life of this world. It rises and flourishes, and then suddenly it withdraws and turns over. It falls to pieces, or a person dies. Based on this, what you possess from this world will either leave you, or you will leave it. There is no third option.

"But in the Hereafter (there is) a severe torment (for the disbelievers, evil-doers), and (there is) forgiveness from Allah and (His) Good Pleasure (for the believers, good-doers)..." There is a severe punishment for the person influenced by the life of this world. The life of this world is only play and amusement, pomp and mutual boasting among you. Allah's Pleasure is with the person who prefers the Hereafter to the life of this world.

Allah says:

بَلْ تُؤْثِرُونَ الْحَيَاةَ الدُّنْيَا وَالآخِرَةُ خَيْرٌ وَأَبْقَى

"Nay, you prefer the life of this world, although the Hereafter is better and more lasting." (Al-A'la: 16-17)

"The life of this world is only a deceptive enjoyment." Included in this verse is everything in this *dunya*. It deceives the person for a period

of time, then vanishes. This world deceives its inhabitant, and then he dies.

عَنْ سَهْلٍ قَالَ سَمِعْتُ النَّبِيَّ ـ صلى الله عليه وسلم ـ يَقُولُ : مَوْضِعُ سَوْطٍ فِى الْجَنَّةِ خَيْرٌ مِنَ الدُّنْيَا وَمَا فِيهَا ، وَلَغَدْوَةٌ فِى سَبِيلِ اللَّهِ أَوْ رَوْحَةٌ خَيْرٌ مِنَ الدُّنْيَا وَمَا فِيهَا

Sahl *radi Allahu anhu* narrated that he heard the Prophet *sallAllahu 'alayhi wa salam* say, *"A small place equal to an area occupied by a whip in Paradise is better than the whole world and whatever is in it; and undertaking a journey for Allah's cause is better than the whole world and whatever is in it."*[3]

Explanation

"A small place equal to an area occupied by a whip in Paradise" is known. However, if this wording is correct, this "small place" is referring to the space occupied by a voice—and Allah knows best. What's implied is the area within reach of the voice.

A whip is a stick about one meter (approximately three feet) in length. This whip is better than the world and everything in it—and it isn't only better than the world you live in, or the world the people live in during your lifetime. This whip is superior to the world from its beginning to its end, and greater than all this world's wealth, castles, high-rise buildings and so forth.

---

[3] (5936)

5

Be in this world as if you are a stranger or traveler

قَوْلِ النَّبِيِّ- صلى الله عليه وسلم كُنْ فِى الدُّنْيَا كَأَنَّكَ غَرِيبٌ ، أَوْ عَابِرُ سَبِيلٍ

The Prophet *salAllahu 'alayhi wa sallam* said, *"Be in this world as if you were a stranger or a traveler."* [4]

Explanation

The Prophet *salAllahu 'alayhi wa sallam* grabbed ibn 'Umar by his shoulder in order to get his attention, when he said "stranger or traveler." The difference between a stranger and a traveler is that a stranger resides in a country that isn't his, while a traveler passes through a land. The meaning of the order is: do not take this world as your residence.

There are three types of people: a settler, a traveler, and an expatriate. The expatriate is a stranger.

The Prophet *salAllahu 'alayhi wa sallam* said, "Be in this world as if you were a stranger…" This means you should behave as if you're living in a place that isn't your home. A "traveler" is a wayfarer. The third person is a settler; you should not live like him, because this world isn't your homeland.

This advice had an effect on ibn 'Umar. Consequently, he said, "When evening comes, don't expect to live until the morning. And when you wake up in the morning, don't expect to live until the evening. Perform righteous deeds and don't delay them in the morning until later in the day."

---

[4] (5937)

Also, don't delay performing good deeds in the last part of the day until the morning. You don't know if you will live until the next day, so you must do good deeds and never desert them."

Hope and hoping for too much Dunya

زُحْزِحَ عَنِ النَّارِ وَأُدْخِلَ الْجَنَّةَ فَقَدْ فَازَ وَما الْحَيَاةُ الدُّنْيَا إِلاَّ مَتَاعُ الْغُرُورِ

And whoever is removed away from the Fire and admitted to Paradise, he indeed is successful. The life of this world is only the enjoyment of deception (a deceiving thing). (Aal-'Imran: 185)

ذَرْهُمْ يَأْكُلُواْ وَيَتَمَتَّعُواْ وَيُلْهِهِمُ الأَمَلُ فَسَوْفَ يَعْلَمُونَ

Leave them to eat and enjoy, and let them be preoccupied with (false) hope. They will come to know! (Al-Hijr: 3)

Explanation

"And whoever is removed from the Fire and admitted to Paradise, he indeed is successful." Indeed everything Allah says is true. This verse says success isn't winning something in this world. The only triumph is to be removed from the Fire and admitted to Paradise.

The Prophet *salAllahu 'alayhi wa sallam* said,

فَمَنْ أَحَبَّ أَنْ يُزَحْزَحَ عَنِ النَّارِ وَيَدْخُلَ الْجَنَّةَ فَلْتَأْتِهِ مَنِيَّتُهُ وَهُوَ يُؤْمِنُ بِاللهِ وَالْيَوْمِ الآخِرِ وَلْيَأْتِ إِلَى النَّاسِ الَّذِى يُحِبُّ أَنْ يُؤْتَى إِلَيْهِ

"Whoever would like to be delivered from Hell and enter Paradise, let him die believing in Allah and the Last Day, and let him treat people the way he would like to be treated." (Muslim, 4882)

This is among the reasons for being saved from Hell and entered into Paradise.

"Leave them to eat and enjoy, and let them be preoccupied with (false) hope. They will come to know!" These words are a threat to those distracted by this life. Leave those who deny Allah and eat from His

bounty. They say, "Tomorrow I will repent; I will repent tomorrow."
When death comes they will realize the reality.

عَنْ عَبْدِ اللَّهِ ـ رضى الله عنه ـ قَالَ خَطَّ النَّبِيُّ ـ صلى الله عليه وسلم ـ خَطًّا
مُرَبَّعًا ، وَخَطَّ خَطًّا فِى الْوَسَطِ خَارِجًا مِنْهُ ، وَخَطَّ خُطَطًا صِغَارًا إِلَى هَذَا الَّذِى
فِى الْوَسَطِ ، مِنْ جَانِبِهِ الَّذِى فِى الْوَسَطِ وَقَالَ » هَذَا الإِنْسَانُ ، وَهَذَا أَجَلُهُ مُحِيطٌ
بِهِ ـ أَوْ قَدْ أَحَاطَ بِهِ ـ وَهَذَا الَّذِى هُوَ خَارِجٌ أَمَلُهُ ، وَهَذِهِ الْخُطَطُ الصِّغَارُ
الأَعْرَاضُ ، فَإِنْ أَخْطَأَهُ هَذَا نَهَشَهُ هَذَا ، وَإِنْ أَخْطَأَهُ هَذَا نَهَشَهُ هَذَا

Narrated Abdullah *radi Allahu 'anhu*: The Prophet *salAllahu 'alayhi
wa sallam* drew a square and then drew a line in the middle of it and
extended it outside the square and then drew several small lines attached
to that central line and said, *"This is the human being, and this (square)
is his lease of life surrounding him on all sides, and this line outside the
square is hope, and the small lines are the calamities and troubles. And if
one misses him, another will overtake him, and if the other misses him, a
third will overtake him."*[5]

Explanation

The Prophet *salAllahu 'alayhi wa sallam* gave an example in this hadeeth when he drew the square. He drew a line in the middle of the
square that extended beyond it. Then he drew lines around the square.
These lines represented man's desire for a longer life than he's been
decreed. The human being's hope is longer than what Allah has willed for
him in this square. He's surrounded by it and can't come out of it. How-

[5] (5938)

9

ever, his wish extends far. An individual wishes to live twenty years longer but only lives a month longer.

Hope extends beyond the boundary of the square. A person's lifespan is surrounded by all four corners. The calamities are on the outside of the square on the left and the right. If he's safe from one, another will catch him and all his hopes will fail.

Therefore, we must make use of the appointed time of life before our death. As for hope, it's farfetched and unlikely. How many people hope to have lunch and dinner with his family, but don't have that? And Allah's aide is sought.

When someone reaches sixty years old he has no right from Allah for a new lease on life

أَوَلَمْ نُعَمِّرْكُمْ مَا يَتَذَكَّرُ فِيهِ مَنْ تَذَكَّرَ وَجَاءَكُمُ النَّذِيرُ

Did We not give you lives long enough that whoever would receive admonition could receive it? And the warner came to you. (Fatir: 37)

عَنْ أَبِي هُرَيْرَةَ عَنِ النَّبِيِّ صَلَّى اللَّهُ عَلَيْهِ وَسَلَّمَ قَالَ أَعْذَرَ اللَّهُ إِلَى امْرِئٍ أَخَّرَ
أَجَلَهُ حَتَّى بَلَّغَهُ سِتِّينَ سَنَةً

Narrated Abu Hurairah *radi Allahu 'anhu*: The Prophet *salAllahu 'alayhi wa sallam* said, *"Allah will not accept the excuse of any person whose natural death is delayed till he is sixty years of age."* [6]

Explanation

" Did We not give you lives long enough that whoever would receive admonition could receive it? And the warner came to you." In this verse, Allah condemns the people in Hell. The proof has been established against them from two angles.

The first angle is that of the universe and man's existence.

The second angle is that of Allah's religion.

In reference to the universe and man's existence, Allah gave them a period during which to live. They reached a certain stage and an admonition came to them. Death didn't concern them, so they said, "By Allah, we weren't given enough time to receive the admonition," when in fact they were given time.

---

[6] (5940)

11

One learns from calamities. All mishaps and calamities must be a religious exhortation for the heart because these trials admonish it. For that reason, Allah says:

$$\text{ظَهَرَ الْفَسَادُ فِي الْبَرِّ وَالْبَحْرِ بِمَا كَسَبَتْ أَيْدِي النَّاسِ لِيُذِيقَهُم بَعْضَ الَّذِي عَمِلُوا لَعَلَّهُمْ يَرْجِعُون}$$

"Evil has appeared on land and sea because of what the hands of men have earned, that He may make them taste a portion of that which they have done." (Ar-Rum: 41)

The angle of religion is the revealed law of Islam. Allah says, *"A warner came to you."* This refers to the Messenger and addresses all nations. The warner for this nation is Muhammad ibn 'Abdullah ibn 'Abdul Mutalib al-Qurayshi, *salAllahu 'alayhi wa sallam*. Every preceding generation of people had bearers of glad tidings and admonitions, and the proof has been established against them.

This is a strong censure of them, increasing their pain and sorrow, and we seek refuge in Allah from it.

They say, "What a pity—how unfortunate we are! How did we not take heed? The warner came to us and we had a long life during which there were lessons and spiritual counsel to learn from."

"Allah will not accept the excuse…" Allah put man to the test, gave him a long life, and during his life there was an excuse: the proof Allah gave him while he was alive. Now he has no excuse with Allah (after his death).

The deed done seeking Allah's countenance

عَنْ أَبِى هُرَيْرَةَ أَنَّ رَسُولَ اللَّهِ ـ صلى الله عليه وسلم ـ قَالَ « يَقُولُ اللَّهُ تَعَالَى
مَا لِعَبْدِى الْمُؤْمِنِ عِنْدِى جَزَاءٌ ، إِذَا قَبَضْتُ صَفِيَّهُ مِنْ أَهْلِ الدُّنْيَا ، ثُمَّ احْتَسَبَهُ إِلاَّ
الْجَنَّةُ

Narrated Abu Hurairah *radi Allahu 'anhu*: Allah's Messenger *salAllahu 'alayhi wa sallam* said, "*Allah says, I have nothing to give but Paradise as a reward to My slave if I cause his dear friend to die and he remains patient and hopes for My reward.*"(5944)

Explanation

In this statement of the Prophet *salAllahu 'alayhi wa sallam*, "hopes" means looking forward to a reward in the Hereafter. This is similar to the *hadeeth* found in Sahih Al-Bukhari. The Prophet *salAllahu 'alayhi wa sallam* said, "The person who fasts in Ramadhan with faith seeking Allah's reward." This word, *Ihtisaaban* (احتسابا) is taken from the word *hisaab* (الحساب). It refers to seeking an exchange for an account of deeds.

"Dear friend" refers here to a true friend and companion, like the son, daughter, father, mother, and so on.

The Warning about worldly pleasures, amusements and competing against each other for enjoyment thereof

أَنَّ عَمْرُو بْنَ عَوْفٍ وَهُوَ حَلِيفٌ لِبَنِي عَامِرِ بْنِ لُؤَيٍّ كَانَ شَهِدَ بَدْرًا مَعَ رَسُولِ اللَّهِ صَلَّى اللَّهُ عَلَيْهِ وَسَلَّمَ أَخْبَرَهُ أَنَّ رَسُولَ اللَّهِ صَلَّى اللَّهُ عَلَيْهِ وَسَلَّمَ بَعَثَ أَبَا عُبَيْدَةَ بْنَ الْجَرَّاحِ إِلَى الْبَحْرَيْنِ يَأْتِي بِجِزْيَتِهَا وَكَانَ رَسُولُ اللَّهِ صَلَّى اللَّهُ عَلَيْهِ وَسَلَّمَ هُوَ صَالَحَ أَهْلَ الْبَحْرَيْنِ وَأَمَّرَ عَلَيْهِمْ الْعَلَاءَ بْنَ الْحَضْرَمِيِّ فَقَدِمَ أَبُو عُبَيْدَةَ بِمَالٍ مِنْ الْبَحْرَيْنِ فَسَمِعَتْ الْأَنْصَارُ بِقُدُومِهِ فَوَافَقْتُهُ صَلَاةَ الصُّبْحِ مَعَ رَسُولِ اللَّهِ صَلَّى اللَّهُ عَلَيْهِ وَسَلَّمَ فَلَمَّا انْصَرَفَ تَعَرَّضُوا لَهُ فَتَبَسَّمَ رَسُولُ اللَّهِ صَلَّى اللَّهُ عَلَيْهِ وَسَلَّمَ حِينَ رَآهُمْ وَقَالَ أَظُنُّكُمْ سَمِعْتُمْ بِقُدُومِ أَبِي عُبَيْدَةَ وَأَنَّهُ جَاءَ بِشَيْءٍ قَالُوا يَا رَسُولَ اللَّهِ قَالَ فَأَبْشِرُوا وَأَمِّلُوا مَا يَسُرُّكُمْ فَوَاللَّهِ مَا الْفَقْرَ أَخْشَى عَلَيْكُمْ وَلَكِنْ أَخْشَى عَلَيْكُمْ أَنْ تُبْسَطَ عَلَيْكُمْ الدُّنْيَا كَمَا بُسِطَتْ عَلَى مَنْ كَانَ قَبْلَكُمْ فَتَنَافَسُوهَا كَمَا تَنَافَسُوهَا وَتُلْهِيَكُمْ كَمَا أَلْهَتْهُمْ.

Narrated Amr bin Auf, an ally of the tribe of Bani 'Amir bin Lu'ai and one of those who witnessed the battle of Badr with Allah's Messenger: Allah's Messenger sent Abu 'Ubaidah bin Al-Jarrah to Bahrain to collect the *jizyah* (tax). Allah's Messenger *salAllahu 'alayhi wa sallam* had concluded a peace treaty with the people of Bahrain and appointed Al-'Ala bin Al-Hadrami as their chief. Abu 'Ubaidah arrived from Bahrain with the money. The Ansaar heard of Abu 'Ubaidah's arrival, which coincided with the Fajr prayer led by Allah's Messenger. When the Prophet *salAllahu 'alayhi wa sallam* finished the prayer, they came to him. Allah's Messenger smiled when he saw them and said, *"I think you have heard of the arrival of Abu 'Ubaidah, and that he has brought something."* They replied, "Yes, O Allah's Messenger!" He said, *"Have the good news and hope for what will please you. By Allah, I am not afraid that you will become poor, but I am afraid that worldly wealth will be given to you in abundance as it was given to those nations before, and you will start competing with each other for it as the previous nations competed for it, and then it will divert you as it diverted them." (5945)*

Explanation

Included in this *hadeeth* is a warning about worldly pleasures and competing against each other to obtain them. Unfortunately, the life of this world has become everyone's concern. People have begun to give importance only to worldly amusements, its comfort and luxury. Rarely do you find anyone talking about religious activities, although Islamic activities are necessary for the Muslims. Instead, Muslims boast about the luxurious things available on earth and what they possess of it. This is what the Prophet *salAllahu 'alayhi wa sallam* feared.

" I am not afraid that you will become poor..." Arrogance, conceit, and turning away from Allah isn't produced by poverty. No doubt a person is distracted at times while seeking subsistence and livelihood. However, if his intention is pure, his search for provision can become worship.

"But I am afraid that worldly wealth will be given to you in abundance as it was given to those nations before..." These worldly riches will be vast and plentiful.

" and you will start competing each other for it as the previous nations competed for it..." You will be diverted the same way they were.

This fear of the Prophet *salAllahu 'alayhi wa sallam* has been realized. We have begun to compete for this *dunya* the same way the disbelievers compete. Many Muslims are only worried about their homes, cars, clothes, gardens, etc.

The statement of Allah, "O mankind! Verily the promise of Allah is true."

يَا أَيُّهَا النَّاسُ إِنَّ وَعْدَ اللَّهِ حَقٌّ فَلَا تَغُرَّنَّكُمُ الْحَيَاةُ الدُّنْيَا وَلَا يَغُرَّنَّكُمْ بِاللَّهِ الْغَرُورُ إِنَّ الشَّيْطَانَ لَكُمْ عَدُوٌّ فَاتَّخِذُوهُ عَدُوًّا إِنَّمَا يَدْعُو حِزْبَهُ لِيَكُونُوا مِنْ أَصْحَابِ السَّعِيرِ

Allah says: "*O mankind! Verily, the promise of Allah is true. So don't let this present life deceive you, and don't let the chief deceiver deceive you about Allah. Surely, Satan is an enemy to you, so treat him as an enemy. He only invites his followers so they can become dwellers of the blazing fire.*" (Fatir: 5-6)

Explanation

"*O mankind! Verily the promise of Allah is true*" This speech is addressed to people in general, including the disbelievers. Allah is speaking to everyone in this verse because the life of this world deceives both Muslims and kuffar.

"*The promise of Allah is true…*" Included in this verse is Allah's promise to the people who do righteous deeds, and Allah's threat to the disbelievers.

"*So don't let this present life deceive you…*" Don't let this lowly life mislead you. The life of this world is delusive and deceptive. The meaning for the word *dunya* is explained in Allah's words:

زُيِّنَ لِلنَّاسِ حُبُّ الشَّهَوَاتِ مِنَ النِّسَاءِ وَالْبَنِينَ وَالْقَنَاطِيرِ الْمُقَنْطَرَةِ مِنَ الذَّهَبِ وَالْفِضَّةِ وَالْخَيْلِ الْمُسَوَّمَةِ وَالْأَنْعَامِ وَالْحَرْثِ ذَلِكَ مَتَاعُ الْحَيَاةِ الدُّنْيَا

"*Beautified for men is the love of things they covet: women, children, much of gold and silver, branded beautiful horses, cattle and well-tilled land. This is the pleasure of the present world's life…*" (Aal-Imran: 14)

16

"And don't let the chief deceiver deceive you about Allah..." The chief deceiver is Shaytaan. This comes from the verse, *"Verily Shaytaan is your enemy."*

"Surely, Satan is an enemy to you, so treat him as an enemy." This is a message and a command from Allah to make the devil our true enemy. If we consider him our enemy, he can't mislead us. Your foe will never command you to something that is in your best interest. What's more, your adversary can never prohibit you from something that is harmful for you. Your enemy will only prevent you from what benefits you and order you to do things that harm you. This is why Allah says, "He only invites his followers so they can become dwellers of the blazing fire."

Based on this verse, we are able to know Shaytaan's commands: everything resulting in a sin or punishment is his order.

Question: How do we distinguish between Shaytaan's instruction and the baser self of Man that incites evil?

Answer: The baser self that incites evil takes its counsel from Shaytaan. This soul orders the person with the instructions that Shaytaan gives.

The righteous people will die

عَنْ مِرْدَاسٍ الْأَسْلَمِيِّ قَالَ قَالَ النَّبِيُّ صَلَّى اللهُ عَلَيْهِ وَسَلَّمَ يَذْهَبُ الصَّالِحُونَ
الْأَوَّلُ فَالْأَوَّلُ وَيَبْقَى حُفَالَةٌ كَحُفَالَةِ الشَّعِيرِ أَوْ التَّمْرِ لَا يُبَالِيهِمْ اللهُ بَالَةً.

Narrated Mirdas Al-Aslami *radi Allahu 'anhu*: The Prophet *salAllahu 'alayhi wa sallam* said, *"The righteous people will die in succession, one after the other, and there will remain useless people like the useless husks of barley seeds or bad dates, and Allah will not care the least for them."*[7]

Explanation

This is similar in meaning to a previous hadeeth, "The best people are those in my generation, then those who follow them…" The righteous people will die one after the other and only the dregs of society will remain, like the useless husks of barley seeds.

"…Allah will not care for them the least" means He won't have any concern about those who punish and torture them, as they aren't worthy of Allah's concern.

---

[7] (5945)

The trial of wealth should be avoided

أَنَسُ بْنُ مَالِكٍ أَنَّ رَسُولَ اللَّهِ صَلَّى اللَّهُ عَلَيْهِ وَسَلَّمَ قَالَ لَوْ أَنَّ لِابْنِ آدَمَ وَادِيًا
مِنْ ذَهَبٍ أَحَبَّ أَنْ يَكُونَ لَهُ وَادِيَانِ وَلَنْ يَمْلَأَ فَاهُ إِلَّا التُّرَابُ وَيَتُوبُ اللَّهُ عَلَى مَنْ
تَابَ

Narrated Anas bin Malik *radi Allahu 'anhu*: Allah's Messenger *salAllahu 'alayhi wa sallam* said, *"If Adam's son had a valley full of gold, he would like to have two valleys, for nothing fills his mouth except dust. And Allah forgives him who repents to Him and begs His pardon."(5959)*

Explanation

Every *hadeeth* in this chapter has the same meaning. The human being never stops craving wealth. If he had two valleys of gold, he would desire a third. If he had three valleys of gold, he would wish for a fourth, and so on.

"... for nothing fills his mouth except dust..." He dies and is buried in the dirt, not that he can fulfill his hunger with dust. Nothing will satisfy his craving until he's buried.

"And Allah forgives him who repents to Him and begs His pardon." If someone has greed and hunger after wealth and he does wrong in seeking it, but repents to Allah, Allah will accept his repentance.

وَقَالَ لَنَا أَبُو الْوَلِيدِ حَدَّثَنَا حَمَّادُ بْنُ سَلَمَةَ عَنْ ثَابِتٍ عَنْ أَنَسٍ عَنْ أُبَيٍّ قَالَ كُنَّا نَرَى هَذَا مِنْ الْقُرْآنِ حَتَّى نَزَلَتْ أَلْهَاكُمْ التَّكَاثُرُ

Ubayy said, "*We considered this a saying from the Qur'aan until the Surah 'The Mutual rivalry for piling up worldly things diverts you.'*"[8]

---

[8] (5959)

The rich who don't spend their wealth on good deeds are in fact poor

مَنْ كَانَ يُرِيدُ الْحَيَاةَ الدُّنْيَا وَزِينَتَهَا نُوَفِّ إِلَيْهِمْ أَعْمَالَهُمْ فِيهَا وَهُمْ فِيهَا لَا يُبْخَسُونَ
أُولَئِكَ الَّذِينَ لَيْسَ لَهُمْ فِي الْآخِرَةِ إِلَّا النَّارُ وَحَبِطَ مَا صَنَعُوا فِيهَا وَبَاطِلٌ مَا كَانُوا
يَعْمَلُونَ

Whoever desires the life of this world and its glitter, to them we shall pay the wages of their deeds therein, and they will have no diminution therein. They are those for whom there is nothing in the Hereafter, but fire and vain are the deeds they did therein. And of no effect is that which they used to do. (Hud: 15-16)

Explanation

" The rich who don't spend their wealth..." They have an abundance of wealth, but don't spend it for Allah's cause; therefore, they are poor on the Day of Judgment. Sometimes a person is wealthy, yet a person less wealthy than him does more with his wealth. Consequently, the second person is rich and the first person is poor on the Day of Judgment.

" Whoever desires the life of this world and its glitter..." "Whoever" is a conditional pronoun with a general meaning including anyone who desires the life of this world and its glitter. Desiring the life of this world means a the desire for a long life. Its glitter includes women, children, a lot of gold and silver, etc.

"... to them we shall pay the wages of their deeds therein..." We give them sufficient actions in this world and reward them for their actions in this world.

"... and they will have no diminution therein. They are those for whom there is nothing in the Hereafter but fire..." For this reason the disbeliever is rewarded for his actions in this life. The *kafir* predominantly lives in this world. This lowly life is his Paradise, luxury and comfort. From this viewpoint, one isn't envied for his luxurious life, but rather for his good deeds.

Whatever one spends from his money will be better for him in the next life

قَالَ عَبْدُ اللَّهِ قَالَ النَّبِيُّ صَلَّى اللَّهُ عَلَيْهِ وَسَلَّمَ أَيُّكُمْ مَالُ وَارِثِهِ أَحَبُّ إِلَيْهِ مِنْ مَالِهِ قَالُوا يَا رَسُولَ اللَّهِ مَا مِنَّا أَحَدٌ إِلَّا مَالُهُ أَحَبُّ إِلَيْهِ قَالَ فَإِنَّ مَالَهُ مَا قَدَّمَ وَمَالُ وَارِثِهِ مَا أَخَّرَ

Narrated 'Abdullah: The Prophet *salAllahu 'alayhi wa sallam* said, *"Who among you considers the wealth of his heirs dearer to him than his wealth?"* They replied, *"O Messenger of Allah! There is none among us but he loves his wealth more."* The Prophet *salAllahu 'alayhi wa sallam* said, *"So his wealth is whatever he spends in Allah's cause during his life, while the wealth of his heirs is whatever he leaves after his death."(5961)*

Explanation

The Prophet *salAllahu 'alayhi wa sallam* spoke the truth. On the Day of Judgment, you will find your wealth in front of you. You can save your money for your heirs by placing it in a safe. The money that benefits you is not placed in it a safe, rather it is spent (for Allah's cause). For this reason, a person should spend his money generously, in a suitable manner.

However, the Prophet *salAllahu 'alayhi wa sallam* said, *"Begin with yourself first, then those who depend on you."* We do not say that someone should spend all his wealth and live poor, especially if he is weak in regard to trusting Allah.

The superiority of being poor

عَنْ عِمْرَانَ بْنِ حُصَيْنٍ رَضِيَ اللَّهُ عَنْهُمَا عَنِ النَّبِيِّ صَلَّى اللَّهُ عَلَيْهِ وَسَلَّمَ قَالَ
اطَّلَعْتُ فِي الْجَنَّةِ فَرَأَيْتُ أَكْثَرَ أَهْلِهَا الْفُقَرَاءَ وَاطَّلَعْتُ فِي النَّارِ فَرَأَيْتُ أَكْثَرَ أَهْلِهَا
النِّسَاءَ

Narrated 'Imran bin Husain: The Prophet *salAllahu 'alayhi wa sallam* said, "*I looked into Paradise and found that the majority of its dwellers were poor people, and I looked into the Hell Fire and found that the majority of its dwellers were women.*"[9]

Explanation

We learn from this *hadeeth* that Paradise and Hellfire are both present. The proof for this is Allah's words:

وَاتَّقُواْ النَّارَ الَّتِي أُعِدَّتْ لِلْكَافِرِينَ

"*And fear the Fire, which is prepared for the disbelievers.*" (Aal-Imran: 131)

وَسَارِعُواْ إِلَى مَغْفِرَةٍ مِّن رَّبِّكُمْ وَجَنَّةٍ عَرْضُهَا السَّمَاوَاتُ وَالأَرْضُ أُعِدَّتْ
لِلْمُتَّقِينَ

"*And march forth on the way to forgiveness from your Lord, and for Paradise as wide as the heavens and the Earth, prepared for the pious.*" (Aal-Imran: 133)

"*I looked into Paradise and found that the majority of its dwellers were poor people...*" Poor people submit to the truth more readily than the rich. They will not be admitted into paradise because of their living

---

[9] (5968)

conditions. There are some rich individuals who are grateful and are more thankful than poor, patient individuals. However, the poor are the highest population of Paradise due to their obedience to the truth more commonly than the rich.

"I looked into the Hell Fire and found that the majority of its dwellers were women." The Prophet *salAllahu 'alayhi wa sallam* explained that the women often curse and are ungrateful towards their husbands. Furthermore, he *salAllahu 'alayhi wa sallam* gave details that women are deficient in their intellect and are a cause for temptation. The Prophet *salAllahu 'alayhi wa sallam* said, *"I haven't left behind me a more harmful trial for the men than the women." (Al-Bukhari 5096)*

The adoption of a middle course

قَالَ سَمِعْتُ مَسْرُوقًا قَالَسَأَلْتُ عَائِشَةَ رَضِيَ اللَّهُ عَنْهَا
أَيُّ الْعَمَلِ كَانَ أَحَبَّ إِلَى النَّبِيِّ صَلَّى اللَّهُ عَلَيْهِ وَسَلَّمَ قَالَتْ الدَّائِمُ قَالَ قُلْتُ فَأَيَّ
حِينٍ كَانَ يَقُومُ قَالَتْ كَانَ يَقُومُ إِذَا سَمِعَ الصَّارِخَ

Narrated Masruq *radi Allahu 'anhu*: I asked Aisha *radi Allahu 'an-humaa*, "What deed was most beloved to the Prophet *salAllahu 'alayhi wa sallam*?" She said, "The regular constant one." I said, "At what time did he get up at night (for the night prayer)? She said, "He used to get up on hearing the crowing of the rooster."[10]

Explanation

The crowing in this *hadeeth* refers to the rooster. In most cases, the rooster's crowing is regulated at a fixed time, in the last third of the night. When it arrives, the rooster begins to crow, in both summer and winter. In the days before watches were invented, people relied on the crow of the rooster and had no need for watches because its crow was always at a fixed time. Hence, when the Prophet *salAllahu 'alayhi wa sallam* heard the rooster, he would get out of bed.

This *hadeeth* illustrates that it is recommended to regularly practice righteous deeds. When a person regularly does good actions it shows he has a desire to practice. On the other hand, the laziness and slackness of a person is proven when he doesn't regularly practice good deeds. Nonetheless, an individual exchanging one action for another he judges to be

---

[10] (5980)

better is not considered someone who abandons the regular practice of good deeds.

عَنْ أَبِي هُرَيْرَةَ رَضِيَ اللَّهُ عَنْهُ قَالَ
قَالَ رَسُولُ اللَّهِ صَلَّى اللَّهُ عَلَيْهِ وَسَلَّمَ لَنْ يُنَجِّيَ أَحَدًا مِنْكُمْ عَمَلُهُ قَالُوا وَلَا أَنْتَ
يَا رَسُولَ اللَّهِ قَالَ وَلَا أَنَا إِلَّا أَنْ يَتَغَمَّدَنِي اللَّهُ بِرَحْمَةٍ سَدِّدُوا وَقَارِبُوا وَاغْدُوا
وَرُوحُوا وَشَيْءٌ مِنَ الدُّلْجَةِ وَالْقَصْدَ الْقَصْدَ تَبْلُغُوا

Narrated Abu Hurairah radi Allahu 'anhu: Allah's Messenger salAlla-hu 'alayhi wa sallam said, *"None of you will be saved from (Hell) by his deeds."* They said, " Even you, O Allah's Messenger?" He said, *"No, even I will not be saved unless and until Allah protects or covers me with His Grace and His Mercy. Therefore, do good deeds properly, sincerely and moderately and worship Allah in the forenoon and in the afternoon and during the part of the night. And always adopt a moderate, regular course whereby you will reach your goal (i.e., Paradise)."*[11]

Explanation

"And always adopt a moderate regular course whereby you will reach your goal (i.e Paradise)." A person shouldn't burden himself, lest he become tired and bored and then leave it.

---

[11] (5982)

"And worship Allah in the forenoon and in the afternoon…" The forenoon is the passing of the morning and the afternoon is the passing into the evening. Worship Allah during part of the night. All of these hours throughout the day shed light on the methodology of life and worship. It's necessary for one to worship in this fashion so that he doesn't create a hardship for himself.

This *hadeeth* proves that actions don't save a person from the fire. However, there is an issue of confusion, as there are texts stating that actions are a reason for being safe from the Fire, such as Allah's words, *"A reward for the things you used to do."* There are other verses with this meaning. Verily, actions are a cause for salvation, not compensation. If actions were compensation, then one of Allah's blessings would suffice all actions. Therefore, actions are a reason for reward, but they are not reimbursed.

To protect one's tongue

عَنْ سَهْلِ بْنِ سَعْدٍ عَنْ رَسُولِ اللَّهِ صَلَّى اللَّهُ عَلَيْهِ وَسَلَّمَ قَالَ مَنْ يَضْمَنْ لِي مَا
بَيْنَ لَحْيَيْهِ وَمَا بَيْنَ رِجْلَيْهِ أَضْمَنْ لَهُ الْجَنَّةَ

Sahl bin Sa'd *radi Allahu 'anhu* narrated: Allah's Messenger *salAllahu 'alayhi wa sallam* said, *"Whoever can guarantee the chastity of what is between his jaw bones and what is between his legs, I guarantee him Paradise."* [12]

Explanation

The Prophet *salAllahu 'alayhi wa sallam* is directing his words here to the believers. If a believer can safeguard the chastity of his tongue and private part, then the Prophet *salAllahu 'alayhi wa sallam* guarantees him Paradise on Allah's behalf. The Prophet *salAllahu 'alayhi wa sallam* never had the ability to guarantee anyone Paradise; however, he promised them based on revelation from Allah, as if he were narrating from Allah.

This *hadeeth* invites the Muslim to protect his tongue from lying, backbiting, slander and so forth.

---

[12] (5933)

29

To be afraid of Allah

عَنْ حُذَيْفَةَ عَنِ النَّبِيِّ صَلَّى اللَّهُ عَلَيْهِ وَسَلَّمَ قَالَ كَانَ رَجُلٌ مِمَّنْ كَانَ قَبْلَكُمْ يُسِيءُ الظَّنَّ بِعَمَلِهِ فَقَالَ لِأَهْلِهِ إِذَا أَنَا مُتُّ فَخُذُونِي فَذَرُّونِي فِي الْبَحْرِ فِي يَوْمٍ صَائِفٍ فَفَعَلُوا بِهِ فَجَمَعَهُ اللَّهُ ثُمَّ قَالَ مَا حَمَلَكَ عَلَى الَّذِي صَنَعْتَ قَالَ مَا حَمَلَنِي إِلَّا مَخَافَتُكَ فَغَفَرَ لَهُ

Narrated Hudhaifa: The Prophet *salAllahu 'alayhi wa sallam* said, *"There was a man amongst the people who was worried about the righteousness of his deeds. Therefore he said to his family, 'If I die, take me and burn my body and throw my ashes into the sea on a hot or windy day.' They did so, but Allah collected his ashes and asked him, 'What made you do what you did?' He replied, 'The only thing that made me do it was that I was afraid of You.' So Allah forgave him."*[13]

Explanation

This man, out of his great fear of Allah decreed by will to be cremated and his ashes scattered. This man did this knowing Allah's ability to reassemble him, but thought that if he was cremated, he would be safe from punishment. Allah reconstructed him and asked him why he had done so. The man replied he did it out the fear of Allah, so Allah forgave him.

The scholars have explained that this man didn't have doubt in Allah's ability; rather, he believed he would be protected from Allah's chastisement. Hence, based on this *hadeeth,* a person isn't a disbeliever when he utters words of disbelief unintentionally.

---

[13] (5999)

There is more proof of this found in the *hadeeth* collected by Muslim:

اللّهُ أَشَدُّ فَرَحًا بِتَوْبَةِ عَبْدِهِ حِينَ يَتُوبُ إِلَيْهِ مِنْ أَحَدِكُمْ كَانَ عَلَى رَاحِلَتِهِ بِأَرْضٍ
فَلَاةٍ فَانْفَلَتَتْ مِنْهُ وَعَلَيْهَا طَعَامُهُ وَشَرَابُهُ فَأَيِسَ مِنْهَا فَأَتَى شَجَرَةً فَاضْطَجَعَ فِى
ظِلِّهَا قَدْ أَيِسَ مِنْ رَاحِلَتِهِ فَبَيْنَا هُوَ كَذَلِكَ إِذَا هُوَ بِهَا قَائِمَةً عِنْدَهُ فَأَخَذَ بِخِطَامِهَا ثُمَّ
قَالَ مِنْ شِدَّةِ الْفَرَحِ اللَّهُمَّ أَنْتَ عَبْدِى وَأَنَا رَبُّكَ. أَخْطَأَ مِنْ شِدَّةِ الْفَرَحِ.

"Allah rejoices more over the repentance of His slave when he repents to Him than one of you, who was on his mount in the wilderness, then he lost his mount. His food and drink are on it, and he despairs of finding it. He goes to a tree and lies down in its shade, having lost hope of finding his mount. While he is like that, it appears in front of him, so he takes hold of its reins and says, in his intense delight, "O Allah, You are my slave and I am your lord," mistakenly because of the degree of his joy."
(Muslim, 6960)

Allah doesn't punish a person in this kind of situation. Additionally, it is a must for a person saying words of *kufr* to have the intention of disbelief to be regarded as a *kafir*, regardless of whether he's serious, joking, or interpreting words.

This *hadeeth* verifies that fear saves a person from Allah's punishment. However something similar has been mentioned in the Qur'aan about Shaytaan:

كَمَثَلِ الشَّيْطَانِ إِذْ قَالَ لِلإِنسَانِ اكْفُرْ فَلَمَّا كَفَرَ قَالَ إِنِّي بَرِيءٌ مِّنكَ إِنِّي أَخَافُ
اللَّهَ رَبَّ الْعَالَمِينَ . فَكَانَ عَاقِبَتَهُمَا أَنَّهُمَا فِي النَّارِ خَالِدَيْنِ فِيهَا وَذَلِكَ جَزَاء
الظَّالِمِينَ.

"Like Shaytaan, when he says to man, 'Disbelieve in Allah.' But when man disbelieves in Allah Shaytaan says, 'Verily, I am free of you; I fear Allah, Lord of everything that exists.'" (Al-Hashr: 16)

Here, the Devil says, "Verily, I am afraid of the Lord of All the Worlds. " However, Shaytaan did not fear Allah due to His Greatness and Exaltation. He was only afraid of his own ruin. He was afraid Allah would destroy him, but not afraid of Allah's Might. Shaytaan didn't draw close to Allah out of fear of Him, and for that reason his fear doesn't benefit him. In fact, the fear of Allah is like man's fear of a lion. A person's fear of a lion does not result in worshipping it or honoring the lion's might.

Question: Was the man who asked to be cremated a Muslim?

Answer: Yes; he only did this out of belief in Allah and certainty He would punish him. Nonetheless, he thought having his ashes scattered would protect him from being punished. He was wrong in this belief.

Question: Allah collected his ashes. Does this refer to the Day of Resurrection?

Answer: No, this collection occurred at the time Allah spoke to him.

Giving up sinful deeds

عَنْ أَبِي بُرْدَةَ عَنْ أَبِي مُوسَى قَالَ قَالَ رَسُولُ اللَّهِ صَلَّى اللَّهُ عَلَيْهِ وَسَلَّمَ مَثَلِي وَمَثَلُ مَا بَعَثَنِي اللَّهُ كَمَثَلِ رَجُلٍ أَتَى قَوْمًا فَقَالَ رَأَيْتُ الْجَيْشَ بِعَيْنَيَّ وَإِنِّي أَنَا النَّذِيرُ الْعُرْيَانُ فَالنَّجَا النَّجَاءَ فَأَطَاعَتْهُ طَائِفَةٌ فَأَدْلَجُوا عَلَى مَهْلِهِمْ فَنَجَوْا وَكَذَّبَتْهُ طَائِفَةٌ فَصَبَّحَهُمُ الْجَيْشُ فَاجْتَاحَهُمْ

Narrated Abu Musa: Allah's Messenger *salAllahu 'alayhi wa sallam* said, "*My example and the example of the message Allah sent me with is that of a man who came to some people and said, 'I have seen with my own eyes the enemy forces and I am a naked warner to you, so save yourself.' A group of them obeyed him and escaped slowly and stealthily at night, and they were safe; another group did not believe him and thus the army overcame them in the morning and destroyed them.*" (6001)

Explanation

This *hadeeth* deals with quitting sinful actions. The human being must hasten to stop sinning. Disobedience is to go against Allah's commands. This can occur either by leaving a commandment or performing a prohibited action.

The Muslim must be upright in carrying out Allah's orders and staying away from His prohibitions. The Prophet *salAllahu 'alayhi wa sallam* gave an example representing himself and the message he came with when he said, "Like a man who came to some people and said, 'I have seen with my own eyes the enemy forces and I am a naked warner to you...'"

"*I have seen with my own eyes...*" This is emphasis. Had the Prophet *salAllahu 'alayhi wa sallam* said, "I have seen" alone, this could have meant, "I know by way of someone or something but I didn't see this enemy with my eyes." However, he said, "*With my own eyes...*" The meaning is similar to Allah's words,

وَلَوْ نَزَّلْنَا عَلَيْكَ كِتَابًا فِي قِرْطَاسٍ فَلَمَسُوهُ بِأَيْدِيهِمْ

"*And even if We had sent down unto you (O Muhammad) a message written on paper, and they could touch it with their hands...*" (Al-An'aam: 7)

"*I am a naked warner...*" Whenever the warning was serious, from the customs of the Arabs was that if he saw danger he would shout, "The encmy, the enemy!" sometimes taking off his clothes. He did this because it was the most effective way to get his people's attention while seeking their salvation.

"*So save yourself...*" You must escape to safety.

"*A group of them obeyed him and escaped slowly and stealthily at night, and they were safe, while another group did not believe him, and thus the army overcame them in the morning and destroyed them.*" Those who obeyed the Messenger of Allah *salAllahu 'alayhi wa sallam* and believed him escaped and were safe. The rest remained behind and the enemy destroyed them.

This *hadeeth* proves that one must rush to obey Allah and His Messenger *salAllahu 'alayhi wa sallam*. And whoever delays observing Allah's commands is in danger.

عَبْدَ اللَّهِ بْنَ عَمْرٍو يَقُولُ قَالَ النَّبِيُّ صَلَّى اللَّهُ عَلَيْهِ وَسَلَّمَ الْمُسْلِمُ مَنْ سَلِمَ الْمُسْلِمُونَ مِنْ لِسَانِهِ وَيَدِهِ وَالْمُهَاجِرُ مَنْ هَجَرَ مَا نَهَى اللَّهُ عَنْهُ

Narrated 'Abdullah ibn 'Amr *radi Allahu 'anhu*: The Prophet *salAllahu 'alayhi wa sallam* said, "*A Muslim is the one who avoids harming Muslims with his tongue and his hands. A* Muhajir *(an Immigrant) is the one who gives up everything Allah has forbidden.*"[14]

Explanation

"*A Muslim is the one who avoids harming Muslims with his tongue and his hands.*" This isn't strictly speaking; this is a definition of the Muslim in regards to the rights of Allah's slaves. It's a general statement implying something specific. The absolute Muslim is the person who submits to Allah outwardly and inwardly.

This *hadeeth* concerns protecting the son of Adam's rights. The one who avoids harming Muslims with his tongue and hands—this is the Muslim.

"*...with his tongue...*" This means the Muslim doesn't attack people with his tongue, insult them with abusive language, or spread gossip to others about them.

"*... and his hands...*" This means the Muslim doesn't commit aggression against others by striking, killing or injuring them, taking their wealth, or otherwise.

"*A* Muhajir *(an Emigrant) is the one who gives up everything Allah has forbidden.*" These words are also general, but carry a specific mean-

---

[14] (6003)

ing. In other words, the person is immigrating to Allah and not from the land of Shirk to the land of Islam. A person migrates to Allah through his actions, not his body. This applies to anyone who forsakes what Allah has forbidden, either through speech or action. Based on this *hadeeth,* we understand that there are various types of immigration and faith.

"... one who gives up everything Allah has forbidden..." If a person were to say, "It doesn't say 'everything the Messenger has forbidden,'" The answer is everything the Messenger has forbidden is everything Allah has forbidden, because the Messenger is Allah's. For that reason Allah says,

مَّنْ يُطِعِ الرَّسُولَ فَقَدْ أَطَاعَ اللَّهَ

" He who obeys the Messenger, has indeed obeyed Allah. " (An-Nisa: 80)

"If you knew what I know"

أَنَّ أَبَا هُرَيْرَةَ رَضِيَ اللَّهُ عَنْهُ كَانَ يَقُولُ

قَالَ رَسُولُ اللَّهِ صَلَّى اللَّهُ عَلَيْهِ وَسَلَّمَ لَوْ تَعْلَمُونَ مَا أَعْلَمُ لَضَحِكْتُمْ قَلِيلًا وَلَبَكَيْتُمْ

كَثِيرًا

Narrated Abu Hurairah *radi Allahu 'anhu*: The Prophet *salAllahu 'alayhi wa sallam* said, *"If you knew what I know, you would laugh less and cry more."*[15]

Explanation

The words in this *hadeeth* are meant to frighten about the punishment. The Prophet *salAllahu 'alayhi wa sallam* said, *"If you knew what I know..."* These words refer to Allah's Sublimity, and not His rules and regulations. Allah's verdicts have been taught to man and no one denies any of them. The Prophet *salAllahu 'alayhi wa sallam* is saying, "If you knew what I know about Allah's Sublimity and Omnipotence..." This knowledge can't be gained except by the person who has a great deal of knowledge.

"...you would laugh less and cry more." This refers to the Prophet's *salAllahu 'alayhi wa sallam* fear of Allah's Power and Punishment on the Day of Judgment. For that reason we say whoever is the most knowledgeable about Allah is the most afraid of Him.

The Prophet *salAllahu 'alayhi wa sallam* was the most filled with fear of Allah. He used to stand at night until his feet swelled up. Muhammad

---

[15] (6004)

salAllahu 'alayhi wa sallam did this because he was a thankful servant of Allah and wanted to express his gratitude to Him. With all of the fear the Prophet *salAllahu 'alayhi wa sallam* possessed, why shouldn't he have been thankful for the blessings Allah gave him?

Hell is surrounded by passions and desires

عَنْ أَبِي هُرَيْرَةَ أَنَّ رَسُولَ اللَّهِ صَلَّى اللَّهُ عَلَيْهِ وَسَلَّمَ قَالَ حُجِبَتْ النَّارُ بِالشَّهَوَاتِ وَحُجِبَتْ الْجَنَّةُ بِالْمَكَارِهِ

Narrated Abu Hurairah *radi Allahu 'anhu*: Allah's Messenger said, *"Hellfire is surrounded by all kinds of desires and passions, while Paradise is surrounded by all kinds of disliked and undesirable things."*[16]

Explanation

The meaning for "surround" is encircled, and the Fire is the place for people who only follow their desires. Among the desires people follow are fornication, sodomy, drinking intoxicants, and spreading mischief and corruption throughout the earth. All of these acts are desires.

These are the desires surrounding Hell. For that reason, most of the people who entered the fire indulged in luxury. This is similar to Allah's words:

"وَأَصْحَابُ الشِّمَالِ مَا أَصْحَابُ الشِّمَالِ. فِي سَمُومٍ وَحَمِيمٍ. وَظِلٍّ مِّن يَحْمُومٍ لاَّ بَارِدٍ وَلا كَرِيمٍ. إِنَّهُمْ كَانُوا قَبْلَ ذَلِكَ مُتْرَفِينَ .

"And those on the Left Hand—who will be those on the Left Hand? In fierce hot wind and boiling water. And shadow of black smoke. (That

---

[16] (6006)

39

shadow) neither cool nor (even) comfortable. Verily before that, they indulged in luxury." (Al-Waqi'ah: 41-46)

The people of desire are those who embark boldly on the things that surround the fire, and consequently enter Hell.

Paradise is the opposite of the Fire. It is surrounded by all kinds of disliked and undesirable things. Since good deeds are disliked by man's baser self, which incites evil, you find many people's souls unwilling toward and detesting good deeds. Nevertheless, good deeds lead one to Paradise, and when one passes beyond the stage of hating good deeds, they become beloved to him and he becomes accustomed to these acts. This is similar to the words of the Prophet *salAllahu 'alayhi wa sallam*:

جعلت قرة عيني في الصلاة

"My comfort has been provided in prayer." (An-Nasa'i, 3392)

Some of the *salaf* used to say, "If the rulers and their children knew our condition, they would beat us with swords."

If a person becomes accustomed to following Allah's commands sincerely with conformity to the Sunnah of the Prophet *salAllahu 'alayhi wa sallam*, obedience will become the most beloved thing to him. But this will not happen for every person at the beginning. Practicing good deeds is generally disliked at first.

This is similar to the speech of the Prophet *salAllahu 'alayhi wa sallam*, *"Perfect the* Wudu, *although it's disliked."* This is an act that raises a person's status and wipes away his sins. "While it's disliked" refers to making it with cold water. A person hates to be splashed by cold water, but makes *wudu* with it seeking Allah's Pleasure. Such an act is a means for a person to enter Paradise. Likewise, when a person travels for Hajj and jihad, he hates this journey. Allah says,

وَعَسَى أَن تَكْرَهُواْ شَيْئًا وَهُوَ خَيْرٌ

"And it may be that you dislike a thing that is good." (Al-Baqarah: 216)

Paradise is closer to all of you than the strap of his shoe

عَبْدِ اللهِ رَضِيَ اللهُ عَنْهُ قَالَ قَالَ النَّبِيُّ صَلَّى اللهُ عَلَيْهِ وَسَلَّمَ الْجَنَّةُ أَقْرَبُ إِلَى أَحَدِكُمْ مِنْ شِرَاكِ نَعْلِهِ وَالنَّارُ مِثْلُ ذَلِكَ

Narrated 'Abdullah *radi Allahu 'anhu*: The Prophet *salAllahu 'alayhi wa sallam* said, *"Paradise is nearer to any of you than the leather strap of his shoe, and so is the Fire."*(6007)

Explanation

After Imam Al-Bukhari *rahimahullah* mentioned in the previous chapter the surroundings of Paradise and Hell, he described how close they are. Paradise and the Fire are both closer to man than the leather strap of his shoe. The Prophet *salAllahu 'alayhi wa sallam* gave an example to illustrate the nearness of the Fire and the Paradise.

The objective of this *hadeeth* is to make people desirous of Paradise. People can attain Paradise by doing the smallest deed. Another purpose of this *hadeeth* is to frighten people about the Fire. Sometimes a person deserves the Hellfire because of the smallest action. Every so often a person says a word that earns him the uppermost Heaven and at times he says a word that lands him in the lowest depths of Hell.

One should always look at the one inferior to him

عَنْ أَبِي هُرَيْرَةَ عَنْ رَسُولِ اللَّهِ صَلَّى اللَّهُ عَلَيْهِ وَسَلَّمَ قَالَ إِذَا نَظَرَ أَحَدُكُمْ إِلَى مَنْ فُضِّلَ عَلَيْهِ فِي الْمَالِ وَالْخَلْقِ فَلْيَنْظُرْ إِلَى مَنْ هُوَ أَسْفَلَ مِنْهُ

Narrated Abu Hurairah *radi Allahu 'anhu:* Allah's Messenger *salAllahu 'alayhi wa sallam* said, *"If anyone of you looked at a person who was made superior to him in property, wealth and appearance, then he should also look at the one who is inferior to him, and to whom he has been made superior."* (6009)

Explanation

This *hadeeth* teaches that when a man looks at anything, he should look at its opposite and compare the two. There are many *ahaadeeth* found in the Sunnah that support this. The Prophet *salAllahu 'alayhi wa sallam* said:

لاَ يَفْرَكْ مُؤْمِنٌ مُؤْمِنَةً إِنْ كَرِهَ مِنْهَا خُلُقًا رَضِيَ مِنْهَا آخَرَ

" A believer shouldn't dislike his believing wife. If he dislikes one trait in her, he likes another one in her." (An-Nasa'i, 3721)

Therefore, whenever you look at a person possessing more wealth than you or more attractive than you, look at someone less wealthy than you and less attractive. By doing this, you will appreciate Allah's Favor and Ability.

Whoever intends to do a good deed or a bad deed

عَنِ ابْنِ عَبَّاسٍ - رضى الله عنهما - عَنِ النَّبِيِّ - صلى الله عليه وسلم - فِيمَا يَرْوِى عَنْ رَبِّهِ عَزَّ وَجَلَّ قَالَ قَالَ » إِنَّ اللَّهَ كَتَبَ الْحَسَنَاتِ وَالسَّيِّئَاتِ ، ثُمَّ بَيَّنَ ذَلِكَ فَمَنْ هَمَّ بِحَسَنَةٍ فَلَمْ يَعْمَلْهَا كَتَبَهَا اللَّهُ لَهُ عِنْدَهُ حَسَنَةً كَامِلَةً ، فَإِنْ هُوَ هَمَّ بِهَا فَعَمِلَهَا كَتَبَهَا اللَّهُ لَهُ عِنْدَهُ عَشْرَ حَسَنَاتٍ إِلَى سَبْعِمِائَةِ ضِعْفٍ إِلَى أَضْعَافٍ كَثِيرَةٍ ، وَمَنْ هَمَّ بِسَيِّئَةٍ فَلَمْ يَعْمَلْهَا كَتَبَهَا اللَّهُ لَهُ عِنْدَهُ حَسَنَةً كَامِلَةً ، فَإِنْ هُوَ هَمَّ بِهَا فَعَمِلَهَا كَتَبَهَا اللَّهُ لَهُ سَيِّئَةً

Narrated Ibn 'Abbaas *radi Allahu 'anhu*: The Prophet *salAllahu 'alayhi wa sallam* narrated from his Lord, *"Allah ordered that the good and the bad deeds be written, and He then showed how to write. If someone intends to do a good deed and he does not do it, Allah will write for him a full good deed; and if he intends to do a good deed and actually does it, Allah will write for him with Him from ten to seven hundred times to many more times; and if someone intends to do a bad deed and he does not do it, Allah will write a full good deed with Him. And if he intends to do a bad deed and actually does it, Allah will write one bad deed (in his account)."*[17]

__Explanation__
"If someone intends…" This applies to the mere idea and intention. The act stops at the person's intention. Hence, the intention to do an act is focused on in this *hadeeth*. There is no action of a slave without the determination to do it. Anyone who intends to do an act and is resolved to perform it is included in this *hadeeth*.

---

[17] (6010)

"If someone intends to do a good deed and he does not do it, then Allah will write for him a full good deed..." This relates to the mere intention to do a good deed. The intention to do a good deed is the decision to do it. This is considered a good act because he didn't intend to do a bad deed or an action of no benefit to waste time.

"... and if he intends to do a good deed and actually does it, then Allah will write for him with Him from ten to seven hundred times to many more times..." There are two levels for good deeds.

1: The person intends to do it.
2: The person intends to perform it and then does it.

There is also a third category, which isn't mentioned in this *hadeeth*. That is, a person intends to perform the act and is prepared to do it, but becomes unable to do it. This is written for him as a complete action as well. He receives a reward for the intention and a reward for the deed if he began it. This is based on Allah's words:

وَمَن يَخْرُجْ مِن بَيْتِهِ مُهَاجِرًا إِلَى اللَّهِ وَرَسُولِهِ ثُمَّ يُدْرِكْهُ الْمَوْتُ فَقَدْ وَقَعَ أَجْرُهُ عَلَى اللَّهِ

"And whoever leaves his home as an immigrant to Allah and His Messenger, and death overtakes him, his reward is then surely incumbent upon Allah. (An-Nisa: 100)

The Prophet *salAllahu 'alayhi wa sallam* said, *"A poor man with no money says to a rich man, 'Spend your wealth for Allah's sake.' The poor man says, 'If I had the wealth that such and such has, I would do what such and such did.'"* He *salAllahu 'alayhi wa sallam* said, *"For his intention, he gets the same reward as that person."*

The mere intention to do a good deed gives the person a complete good deed. However, if he intends to do it but is unable to—especially if he started it—and then he will get the complete reward. If he didn't do it, he will get a reward of ten to seven hundred or more good deeds. These are the three categories of people in regards to actions.

"If someone intends to do a bad deed and he does not do it, then Allah will write a full good deed with Him. And if he intends to do a bad deed and actually does it, then Allah will write one bad deed." The Prophet *salAllahu 'alayhi wa sallam* said completed good deeds are recorded as complete with multiple rewards and completed bad deeds are recorded singly. He *salAllahu 'alayhi wa sallam* did so to prevent the misunderstanding that a person intending to do a bad deed but didn't carry it out would have anything more recorded.

The conditions under which one good deed is written for a person intending to do a bad deed but doesn't are:

1. He has the ability. This is written as a sin for him. And if he embarks on it and then becomes unable to fully complete it, what's recorded is worse than if he only intended to do it.

2. He abandons this act for Allah's pleasure. This person is rewarded for not carrying out this act.

3. The person stays away from this act, not desiring to do it. In this case, he is neither rewarded nor recorded as having committed a sin.

عَنْ أَنَسٍ رَضِيَ اللّٰهُ عَنْهُ قَالَ إِنَّكُمْ لَتَعْمَلُونَ أَعْمَالًا هِيَ أَدَقُّ فِي أَعْيُنِكُمْ مِنْ الشَّعَرِ إِنْ كُنَّا لَنَعُدُّهَا عَلَى عَهْدِ النَّبِيِّ صَلَّى اللّٰهُ عَلَيْهِ وَسَلَّمَ مِنْ الْمُوبِقَاتِ

Anas *radi Allahu 'anhu* said, "You do bad deeds which seem in your eyes as a thin strand of hair, while we used to consider those during the life time of the Prophet *salAllahu 'alayhi wa sallam* as destructive sins."[18]

Explanation

This *hadeeth* deals with the kind of protection that should be sought against minor sins. One must avoid minor sins. Someone might say, "This sin is small and Allah is Oft-Forgiving, Most Merciful." We say, "Be careful of training your soul in this fashion, as these minor sins add up and become a mountain of small stones."

If a person accustoms his soul to minor sins, the major sins will become easy for him. For that reason the scholars said, "The minor sins are a way to major sins. And the majors sins are the means to disbelief."

A person progresses stage by stage until he reaches his highest level in disobedience. It's impermissible for a person to have a low opinion about any sin; such a belief is harmful for his present and future condition.

In the time of the Prophet *salAllahu 'alayhi wa sallam,* people would consider certain actions enormous and see them as being dangerous. However, during the era the Anas lived in after the Prophet *salAllahu*

[18] (6011)

'alayhi wa sallam, people changed so much that words were not considered to be worth anything. A person would backbite and spread tales, not giving any importance to it. Sometimes the match of *fitnah* is ignited by one word, even if the person who said it didn't believe it was a big deal.

This is why Anas *radi Allahu 'anhu* warned against these minor sins.

The results of deeds done depend on the last actions

عَنْ سَهْلِ بْنِ سَعْدٍ السَّاعِدِيِّ قَالَ نَظَرَ النَّبِيُّ صَلَّى اللهُ عَلَيْهِ وَسَلَّمَ إِلَى رَجُلٍ يُقَاتِلُ
الْمُشْرِكِينَ وَكَانَ مِنْ أَعْظَمِ الْمُسْلِمِينَ غَنَاءً عَنْهُمْ فَقَالَ مَنْ أَحَبَّ أَنْ يَنْظُرَ إِلَى رَجُلٍ
مِنْ أَهْلِ النَّارِ فَلْيَنْظُرْ إِلَى هَذَا فَتَبِعَهُ رَجُلٌ فَلَمْ يَزَلْ عَلَى ذَلِكَ حَتَّى جُرِحَ فَاسْتَعْجَلَ
الْمَوْتَ فَقَالَ بِذُبَابَةِ سَيْفِهِ فَوَضَعَهُ بَيْنَ ثَدْيَيْهِ فَتَحَامَلَ عَلَيْهِ حَتَّى خَرَجَ مِنْ بَيْنِ كَتِفَيْهِ
فَقَالَ النَّبِيُّ صَلَّى اللهُ عَلَيْهِ وَسَلَّمَ إِنَّ الْعَبْدَ لَيَعْمَلُ فِيمَا يَرَى النَّاسُ عَمَلَ أَهْلِ الْجَنَّةِ وَإِنَّهُ
لَمِنْ أَهْلِ النَّارِ وَيَعْمَلُ فِيمَا يَرَى النَّاسُ عَمَلَ أَهْلِ النَّارِ وَهُوَ مِنْ أَهْلِ الْجَنَّةِ وَإِنَّمَا
الْأَعْمَالُ بِخَوَاتِيمِهَا

Sahl ibn Sa'd as-Sa'idi *radi Allahu 'anhu*: The Prophet *salAllahu 'alayhi wa sallam* looked at a man fighting against the *mushrikoon,* and he was one of the most competent people fighting on behalf of the Muslims. The Prophet *salAllahu 'alayhi wa sallam* said, *"Let him who wants to look at a man from the dwellers of the Hell Fire look at this man."* Another man followed him until the fighter was injured. Seeking to die quickly, he placed the tip of his sword between his breasts and leaned over it until it passed through his shoulders. The Prophet *salAllahu 'alayhi wa sallam* added, *"A person may do deeds that seem to be the deeds of the people of Paradise while in fact he is from the dwellers of the Fire. Similarly, a person may do deeds that seem to be the deeds of the people of Hell while in fact he is from the dwellers of Paradise. Verily the results of deeds depend on the last actions."* (6012)

Explanation

"The results of deeds depend on the last actions." The Prophet *salAllahu 'alayhi wa sallam* said this because the person might do the deeds of the people of Paradise while he's among the people of Hell, and vice versa. Based on this *hadeeth,* one must be cautious and afraid of doing good deeds all his life until a certain point, and then doing actions like the people of Hell.

In another narration of this *hadeeth,* the Prophet *salAllahu 'alayhi wa sallam* mentioned a man who was very courageous. He didn't come upon any sheep or cattle of the enemy except he killed them. For that reason, the Prophet *sallahu alayhi wa salam* said, "Whoever desires to see a person from the dwellers of Hell, then look at him." This speech was troublesome and hard for the companions to bear. They said, "How can this man be among the dwellers of Hell and he has this characteristic and fights in this fashion?"

Hence, one of the companions said, "By Allah, I will follow him to see how he ends up." Then he witnessed what's mentioned in the *hadeeth.* After all his bravery and fighting in the manner he fought, when he was wounded he placed the tip of his sword between his breasts and leaned over it until it passed through his shoulders and died of this suicide.

Therefore, he *salAllahu 'alayhi wa sallam* said, *"A person may do deeds that seem to be the deeds of the people of Paradise while in fact, he is from the dwellers of the Fire..."* We seek refuge in Allah from this.

"...that seem to be..." This means that what this person manifests contradicts what is hidden inside him. *"Similarly, a person may do deeds that seem to be the deeds of the people of Hell while in fact he is from the dwellers of Paradise..."*

50

The disappearance of trust and moral responsibility

عَنْ أَبِي هُرَيْرَةَ رَضِيَ اللَّهُ عَنْهُ قَالَ قَالَ رَسُولُ اللَّهِ صَلَّى اللَّهُ عَلَيْهِ وَسَلَّمَ إِذَا
ضُيِّعَتُ الْأَمَانَةُ فَانْتَظِرْ السَّاعَةَ قَالَ كَيْفَ إِضَاعَتُهَا يَا رَسُولَ اللَّهِ قَالَ إِذَا أُسْنِدَ
الْأَمْرُ إِلَى غَيْرِ أَهْلِهِ فَانْتَظِرْ السَّاعَةَ

Narrated Abu Hurairah *radi Allahu 'anhu*: Allah's Messenger *salAl-lahu 'alayhi wa sallam* said, "*When* amaanah *is lost, wait for the hour.*" It was said, "How will *amaanah* be lost, O Allah's Messenger?" He said, "*When authority is given to those who do not deserve it, then wait for the hour.*" (6015)

Explanation

Al-Amaanah: Trust and moral responsibility.

The intended meaning of the word "hour" could mean the Day of Judgment or the time when Muslims will be destroyed. In other words, this nation will be destroyed when trust is lost. Even though the Day of Judgment hasn't happened, both meanings are included.

This *hadeeth* proves that in the last days of this world, this nation will become corrupt due to the loss of moral responsibility. This corruption will take place when authority is given to those who don't deserve it because they aren't qualified in general and specific governing matters.

For example, an authoritative position may be given to someone who is irreligious. This person shows favoritism towards his relatives or the rich while in his position, doesn't establish the legal penalties put in place by Allah, oppresses the poor, and so forth. This kind of individual is ineligible for a position of power. W hen he is given authority, wait for the Hour.

Someone may be given authority in the affairs of the Muslims who doesn't judge by the Qur'aan and Sunnah. This type of person isn't fit to lead, so when you witness this kind of man given power, wait for the .

Included in this is a manager not proficient in management or other profession, or someone not properly educated but a close relative or friend of the minister. When he's given a position he's unqualified for by the minister, this is also a loss of trust. In fact, the Prophet *salAllahu 'alayhi wa sallam* mentioned that someone who appoints a person over another more qualified has acted disloyally towards Allah, His Messenger and the believers.

Applying this *hadeeth* to our situation today, one sees trust and moral responsibility has vanished except in those areas Allah has willed, and authority has been given to people who don't deserve it. Hence, we are waiting for either the hour of destruction or the hour of the Day of Judgment. The Prophet *salAllahu 'alayhi wa sallam* has laid down the condition and the result.

Showing off and seeking fame

جُنْدَبًا يَقُولُ قَالَ النَّبِيُّ صَلَّى اللهُ عَلَيْهِ وَسَلَّمَ وَلَمْ أَسْمَعْ أَحَدًا يَقُولُ قَالَ النَّبِيُّ
صَلَّى اللهُ عَلَيْهِ وَسَلَّمَ غَيْرَهُ فَدَنَوْتُ مِنْهُ فَسَمِعْتُهُ يَقُولُ قَالَ النَّبِيُّ صَلَّى اللهُ عَلَيْهِ
وَسَلَّمَ مَنْ سَمَّعَ سَمَّعَ اللهُ بِهِ وَمَنْ يُرَائِي يُرَائِي اللهُ بِهِ

Narrated Jundub: The Prophet *salAllahu 'alayhi wa sallam* said, *"He who lets the people hear of his good deeds intentionally to win their praise, Allah will let the people know his real intention. And the person who does good things in public to show off and to win the praise of the people, Allah will disclose his real intention."* [19]

Explanation

"He who lets the people hear of his good deeds intentionally..." A person says words that seem to draw him closer to Allah, but only to be heard by people and praised by them. Hence, Allah lets his real intention become known; then the people begin talking about him.

"And the person who does good things in public to show off..." Actions are seen and words are heard. A person either says or does something. So whoever says something so people can hear about it and does something so that people can see it, Allah will make his condition known. For this reason, there is a warning against showing off and seeking fame in this *hadeeth*.

---

[19] (6018)

53

Question: Sometimes these feelings befall a person, or come to his mind and he isn't able to repel these thoughts and feelings.

Answer: This is correct. Sometimes the idea of doing things to be seen or heard occurs to an individual and he can't repel them. The cure for this is to say to yourself, "I'm doing this so people can follow me, not praise me."

If you do something so others can take you as an example, showing off vanishes. Then you should feel the burden of responsibility: You are now a leader and you want people to follow you in goodness.

If you obey Shaytaan in his speech, "You are showing off; you aren't doing this act for Allah," you will turn away from this act and your soul will feel the things Shaytaan whispered to you. Allah's aide is sought!